Hal Leonard
GUITAR METHOD
Supplement to Any Guitar Method

EASY POP RHYTHMS
THIRD EDITION

INTRODUCTION

Welcome to *Easy Pop Rhythms*, a collection of 20 pop and rock favorites arranged for easy guitar chord strumming. If you're a beginning guitarist, you've come to the right place. With the songs in this book, you can practice basic chords and strumming patterns—plus learn how to play 20 great tunes!

This book can be used on its own or as a supplement to any guitar method. If you're using it along with the *Hal Leonard Guitar Method*, it coordinates with the skills introduced in Book 1. Use the table of contents on page 3 to see what chords each song contains and to determine when you're ready to play a song.

ISBN 978-0-634-03860-0

7777 W. BLUEMOUND RD. P.O. BOX 13819 MILWAUKEE, WI 53213

Visit Hal Leonard Online at
www.halleonard.com

SONG STRUCTURE

The songs in this book have different sections, which may or may not include the following:

Intro
This is usually a short instrumental section that "introduces" the song at the beginning.

Verse
This is one of the main sections of a song and conveys most of the storyline. A song usually has several verses, all with the same music but each with different lyrics.

Chorus
This is often the most memorable section of a song. Unlike the verse, the chorus usually has the same lyrics every time it repeats.

Bridge
This section is a break from the rest of the song, often having a very different chord progression and feel.

Solo
This is an instrumental section, often played over the verse or chorus structure.

Outro
Similar to an intro, this section brings the song to an end.

ENDINGS & REPEATS

Many of the songs have some new symbols that you must understand before playing. Each of these represents a different type of ending.

1st and 2nd Endings
These are indicated by brackets and numbers. The first time through a song section, play the first ending and then repeat. The second time through, skip the first ending, and play through the second ending.

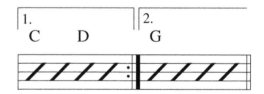

D.S.
This means "Dal Segno" or "from the sign." When you see this abbreviation above the staff, find the sign (𝄋) earlier in the song and resume playing from that point.

al Coda
This means "to the Coda," a concluding section in the song. If you see the words "D.S. al Coda," return to the sign (𝄋) earlier in the song and play until you see the words "To Coda," then skip to the Coda at the end of the song, indicated by the symbol: ⊕.

al Fine
This means "to the end." If you see the words "D.S. al Fine," return to the sign (𝄋) earlier in the song and play until you see the word "Fine."

D.C.
This means "Da Capo" or "from the head." When you see this abbreviation above the staff, return to the beginning (or "head") of the song and resume playing.

CONTENTS

JAMBALAYA
(On the Bayou)

Words and Music by
Hank Williams

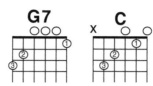

Intro
Moderately

*N.C. = no chord

1.Good-bye

Verse

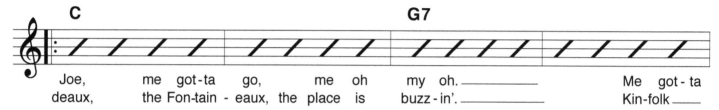

Joe, me got-ta go, me oh my oh. Me got-ta
deaux, the Fon-tain-eaux, the place is buzz-in'. Kin-folk

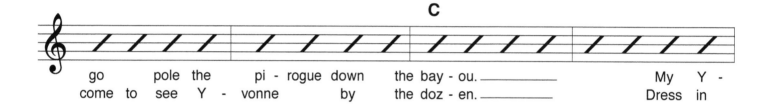

go pole the pi-rogue down the bay-ou. My Y-
come to see Y-vonne by the doz-en. Dress in

vonne, the sweet-est one, me oh, my oh. Son of a
style, and go hog wild, me oh, my oh.

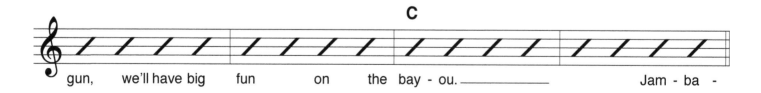

gun, we'll have big fun on the bay-ou. Jam-ba-

%. Chorus

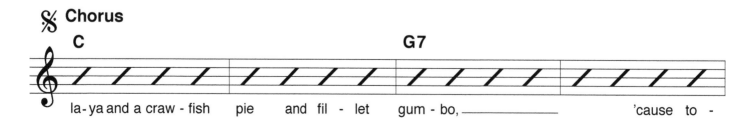

la-ya and a craw-fish pie and fil-let gum-bo, 'cause to-

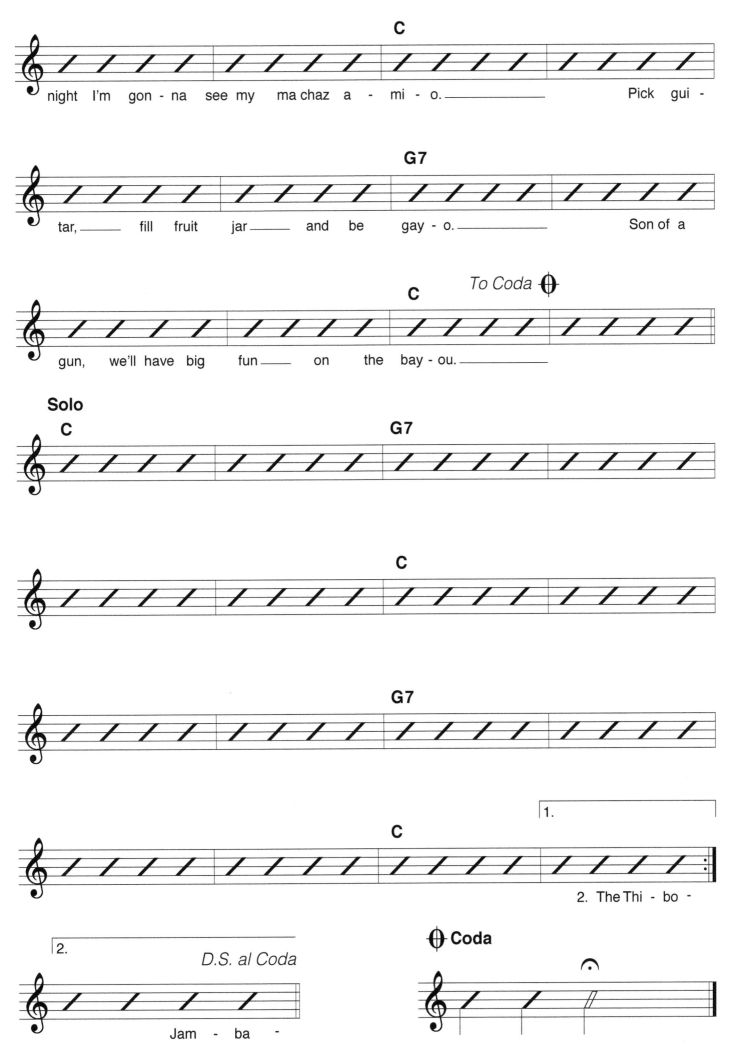

Rock Around the Clock

Words and Music by
Max C. Freedman
and Jimmy DeKnight

Intro
Moderately fast

One, two three o'-clock, four o'-clock rock.

Five, six, sev-en o'-clock, eight o'-clock rock.

Nine, ten, e-lev-en o'-clock twelve o'-clock rock. We're gon-na

D7
rock a-round the clock to-night. 1. Put your

Verse

G
glad rags on, join me, hon.___ We'll
(2.) clock strikes two, three and four,___ if the
(3.) chimes ring five, six and se-ven,
4., 5. *See additional lyrics*

G7
have some fun when the clock strikes one.
band slows down we'll yell for more. } We're gon-na
we'll be right in sev-enth heav-en.

Additional Lyrics

4. When it's eight, nine, ten, eleven too,
   I'll be goin' strong and so will you.
   We're gonna rock around the clock tonight…

5. When the clock strikes twelve, we'll cool off then,
   Start a-rockin' 'round the clock again.
   We're gonna rock around the clock tonight…

WHAT I GOT

Words and Music by Brad Nowell, Eric Wilson,
Floyd Gaugh and Lindon Roberts

Guitar Solo

| D | G | D | G | D | G | D | G |

2. Well, life

Verse

| D | | G | | D | | G |

is too short, so love _ the one you got 'cause you might get run o-ver or you might get shot.

| D | | G | | D | | G |

Nev-er start no stat-ic, I get _ it off my _ chest.   Nev-er had to bat-tle with no bul-let-proof vest.

| D | | G | | D | | G |

Take a small ex-am-ple, a tip from me.   Take all of your mon-ey, give it all to char-i-ty-ty-ty-ty. _

| D | | G | | D | | G |

___ Love's what I got with-in my reach. The   Sub-lime style's still straight from Long Beach.   It

| D | | G | | D | | G |

comes back to you, you're gon-na get what you de-serve. Try and test that; you're bound to get served.

| D | | G | | D | | G |

Love's what I got, don't start a ri-ot.   You   feel it when the dance gets hot,   hot.

Repeat and fade

Chorus

| D | | G | | D | | G |

Lov - in' ___   is what I   got. ___   I said re-mem-ber that. _

9

Bye Bye Love

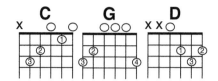

Words and Music by Felice Bryant
and Boudleaux Bryant

Chorus
Moderately fast

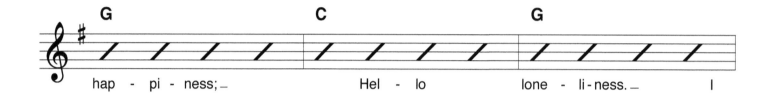

Bye   bye   love;   Bye   bye

hap - pi - ness;—   Hel - lo   lone - li - ness.—   I

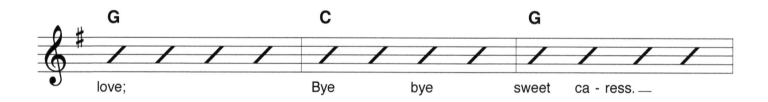

think   I'm   gon - na   cry._____   Bye   bye

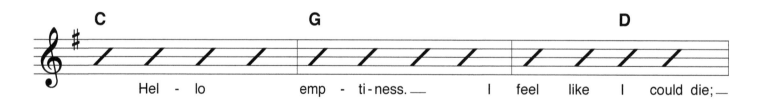

love;   Bye   bye   sweet   ca - ress.—

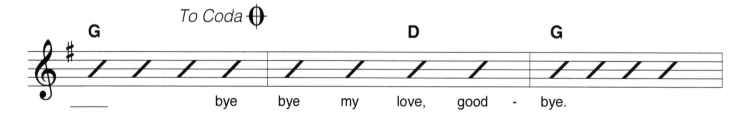

Hel - lo   emp - ti - ness.—   I   feel   like   I   could   die;—

To Coda ⊕

_____   bye   bye   my   love,   good - bye.

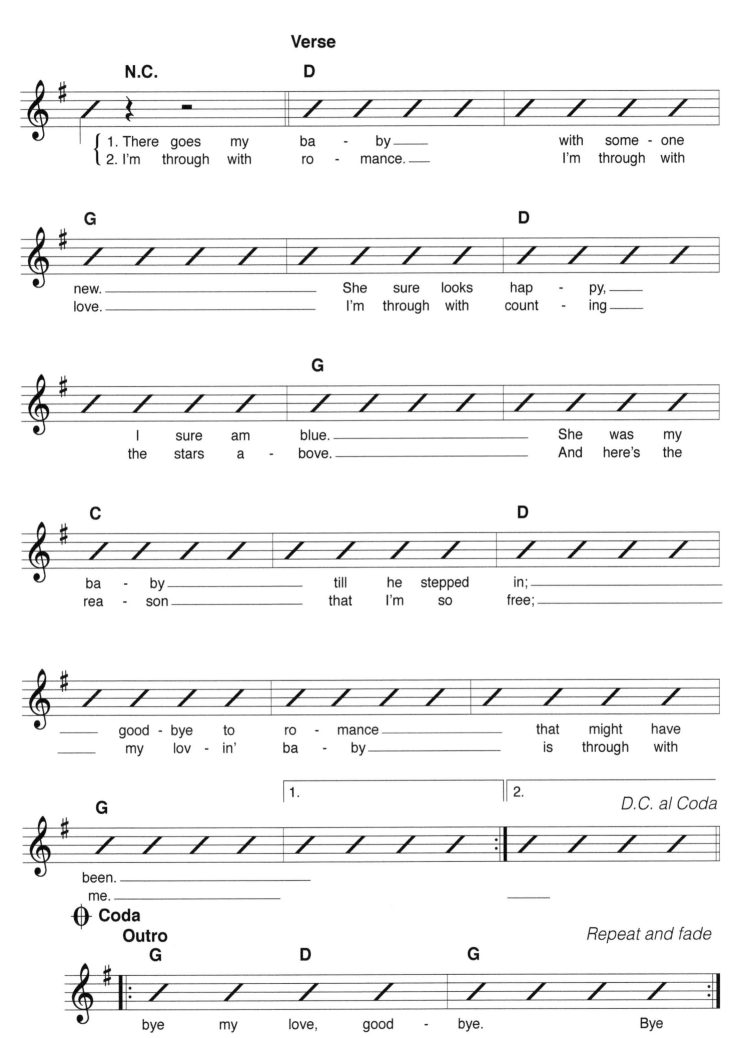

Verse

N.C.　　　　　　D

1. There goes my ba - by _____ with some - one
2. I'm through with ro - mance. _____ I'm through with

G　　　　　　　　　D

new. _____ She sure looks hap - py, ___
love. _____ I'm through with count - ing ___

G

I sure am blue. _____ She was my
the stars a - bove. _____ And here's the

C　　　　　　　　　D

ba - by _____ till he stepped in; ___
rea - son _____ that I'm so free; ___

_____ good - bye to ro - mance _____ that might have
_____ my lov - in' ba - by _____ is through with

1.

been. _____

2.

me. _____

D.C. al Coda

G

🪙 **Coda**
Outro

Repeat and fade

G　　　　　D　　　　　G

bye my love, good - bye. Bye

LOVE ME DO

Words and Music by John Lennon
and Paul McCartney

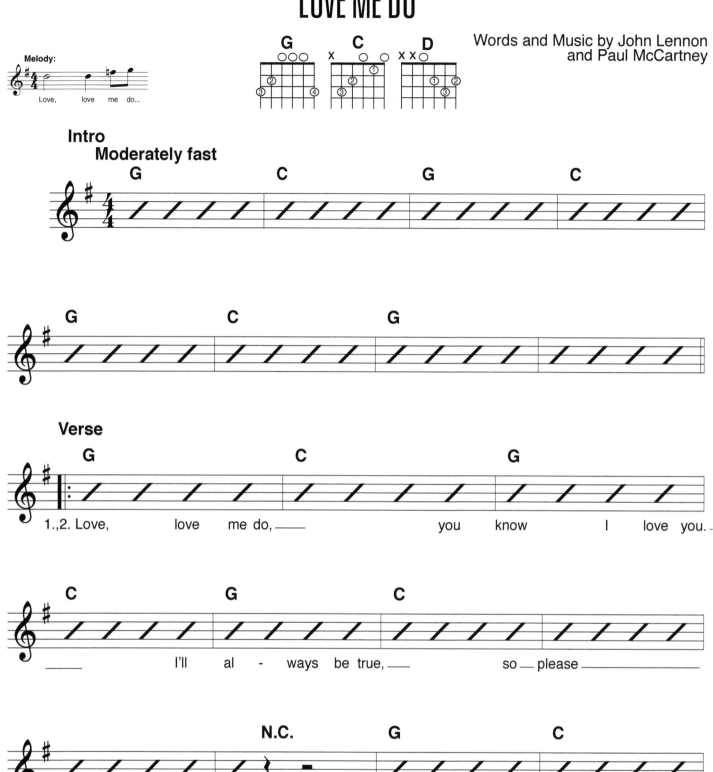

Intro
Moderately fast

G | C | G | C |

G | C | G |

Verse

G | C | G |

1.,2. Love,   love me do, _____   you know   I   love you.

C | G | C |

_____ I'll al - ways be true, _____   so _ please _____

N.C. | G | C |

_____   love me do. _____   Whoa, _ love _

Bridge

G | C | D |

___ me do. _____   Some - one to love,

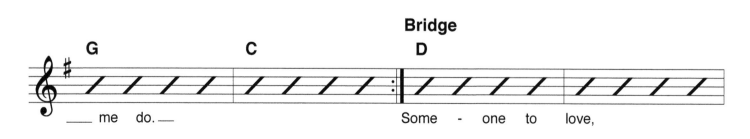

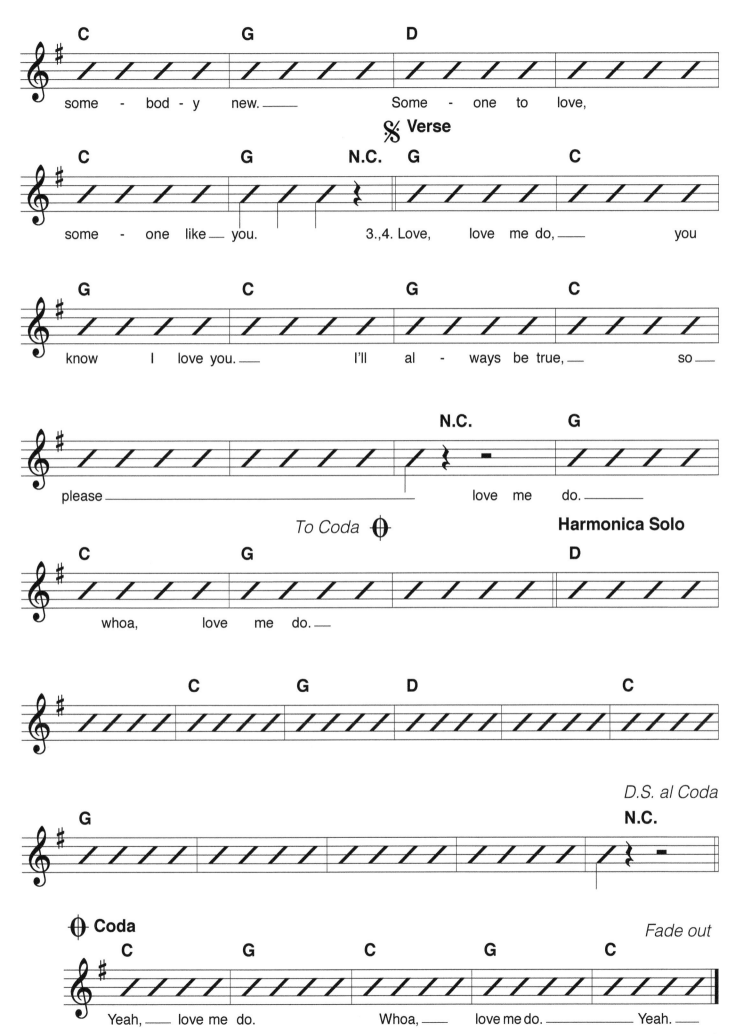

SIMPLE MAN

ALL ALONG THE WATCHTOWER

Words and Music by
Bob Dylan

1.There must be some kind of way out - ta here,
2. No rea - son to get ex - cit - ed,
3. *See additional lyrics*

said the jok - er to the thief.
the thief, he kind - ly spoke.

There's too much con - fu - sion.
There are man - y here a - mong

I can't get no re - lief. ___
who feel that life is but a joke. ___

us

Busi - ness men, they drink my wine.
But you and I, we've been ___ through that,

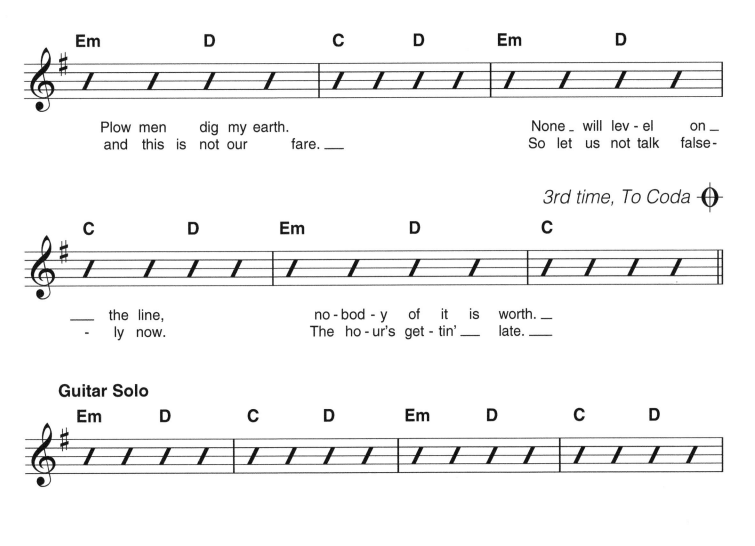

Plow men dig my earth.
and this is not our fare. ___

None _ will lev - el on _
So let us not talk false-

3rd time, To Coda ⊕

___ the line,
- ly now.

no - bod - y of it is worth. _
The ho - ur's get - tin' ___ late. ___

Guitar Solo

2nd time, D.S. al Coda

⊕ **Coda**

Outro-Guitar Solo

Repeat and fade

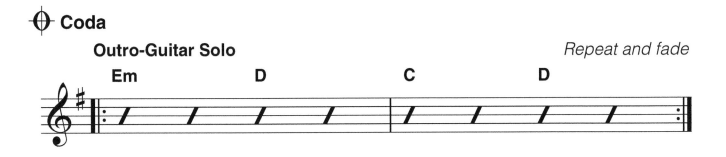

Additional Lyrics

3. Well, all along the watchtower, princes kept the view
   While all the women came and went, barefoot servants, too.
   Outside in the cold distance, a wild cat did growl.
   Two riders were approachin', and the wind began to howl.

WONDERFUL TONIGHT

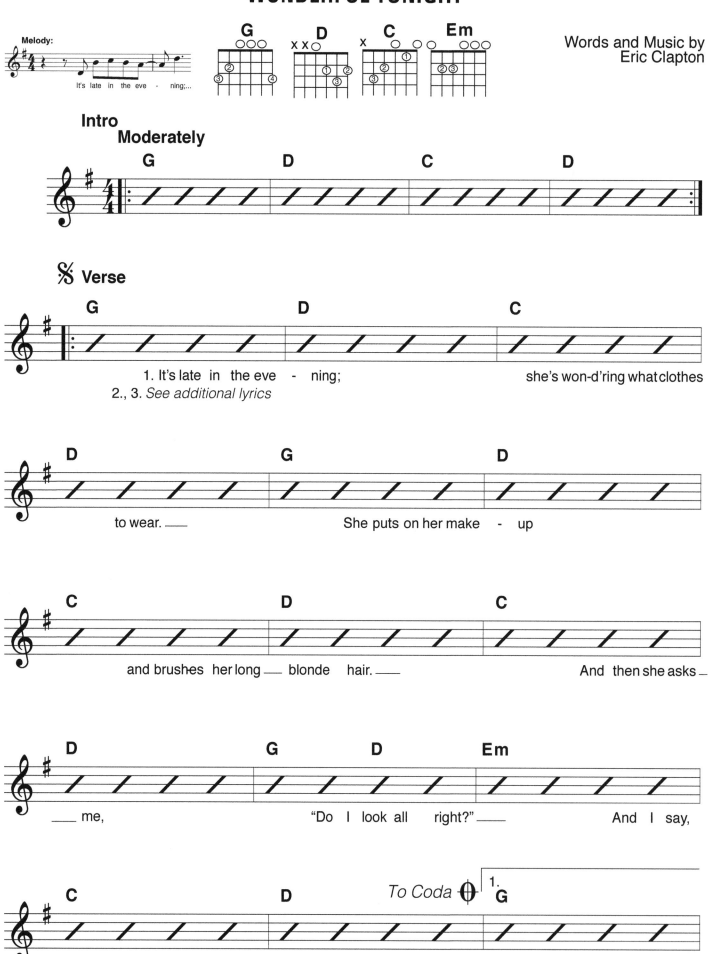

Words and Music by
Eric Clapton

Intro Moderately

| G | D | C | D |

Verse

| G | D | C |

1. It's late in the eve - ning;   she's won-d'ring what clothes
2., 3. *See additional lyrics*

| D | G | D |

to wear. ___   She puts on her make - up

| C | D | C |

and brush-es her long ___ blonde hair. ___   And then she asks ___

| D | G   D | Em |

___ me,   "Do I look all right?" ___   And I say,

| C | D | *To Coda* ⊕ 1. G |

"Yes,   you look won - der - ful ___ to-night." ___

Additional Lyrics

2. We go to a party, and ev'ryone turns to see
This beautiful lady that's walking around with me.
And then she asks me, "Do you feel alright?"
And I say, "Yes, I feel wonderful tonight."

3. It's time to go home now, and I've got an aching head.
So I give her the car keys and she helps me to bed.
And then I tell her, as I turn out the light,
I say, "My darling, you were wonderful tonight."

WAGON WHEEL

Words and Music by
Bob Dylan and Ketch Secor

Melody:

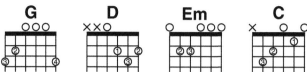

Verse
Moderate shuffle

1. Head-in' down south _ to the land of the pines, _ I'm thumb-in' my way _ out of North _
2. Run-nin' from the cold ___ up in New Eng-land, I was born to be a fid-dler in an
3. *See additional lyrics*

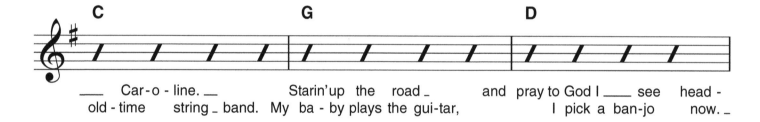

___ Car-o - line. _ Starin' up the road _ and pray to God I ___ see head -
old - time string _ band. My ba - by plays the gui-tar, I pick a ban-jo now. _

- lights.
_____
I made it down the coast in
Oh, north count-ry win-ters keep a

sev - en-teen hours. _ Pick - in' me a bou - quet of dog - wood flowers. _ And I'm a
get - tin' me down. _ Lost my mon - ey play-in' pok - er, so I had to leave town. _ But I

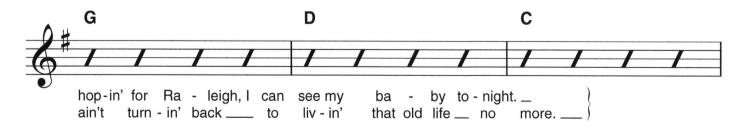

hop-in' for Ra - leigh, I can see my ba - by to - night. _
ain't turn - in' back ___ to liv - in' that old life _ no more. _

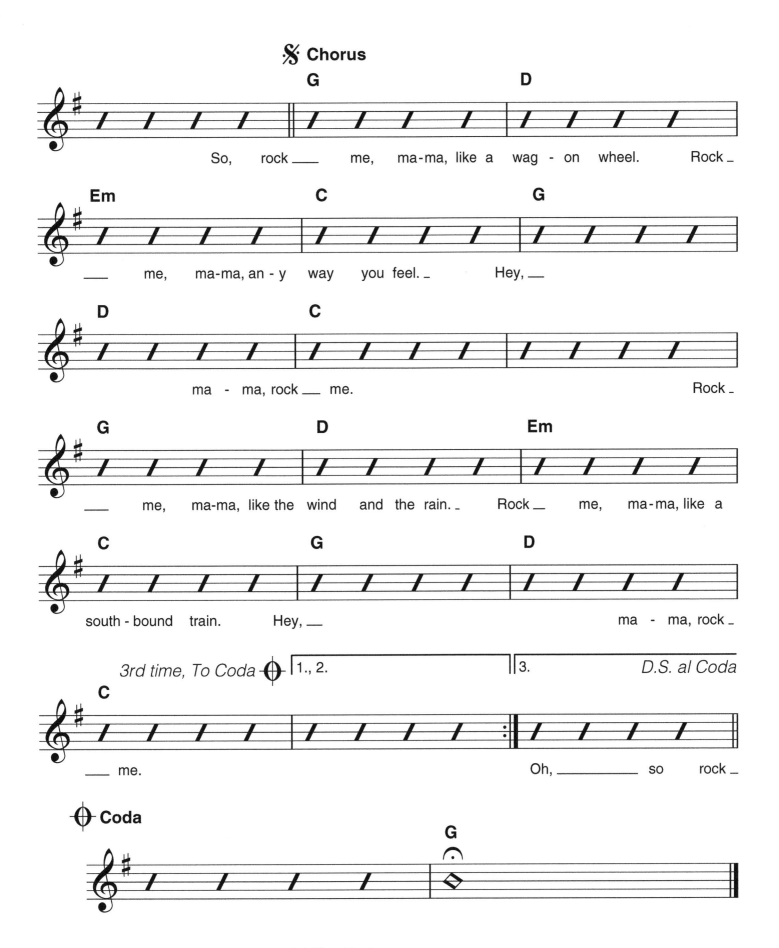

Additional Lyrics

3. Walkin' through the South out of Roanoke,
I caught a trucker out of Philly, had a nice long toke.
But he's a headin' west from the Cumberland Gap to Johnson City, Tennessee.
I got, I gotta move on before the sun.
I hear my baby callin' my name and I know that she's the only one.
And if I die in Raleigh, at least I will die free.

TEACH YOUR CHILDREN

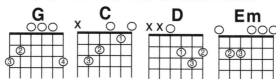

Words and Music by
Graham Nash

Intro
Moderately

Verse

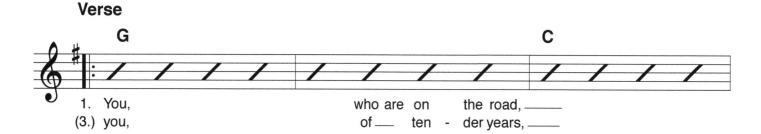

1. You,   who are on   the road, _____
(3.) you,   of ___ ten - der years, _____

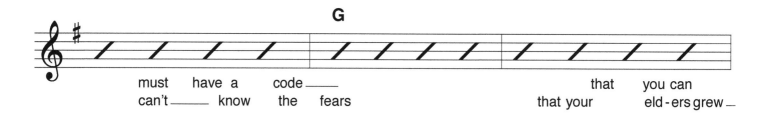

must   have a   code _____   that   you can
can't ___ know   the   fears   that your   eld - ers grew

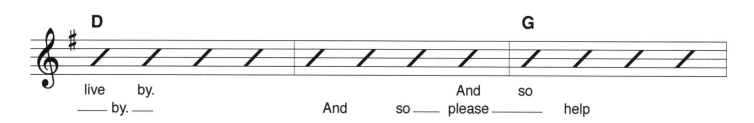

live   by.   And   so
___ by. ___   And   so ___ please _____   help

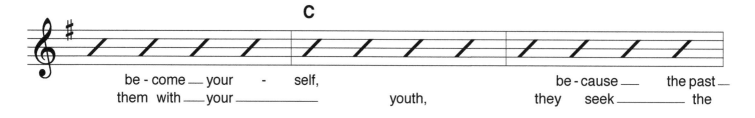

be - come ___ your - self,   be - cause ___ the past
them with ___ your _____   youth,   they   seek _____ the

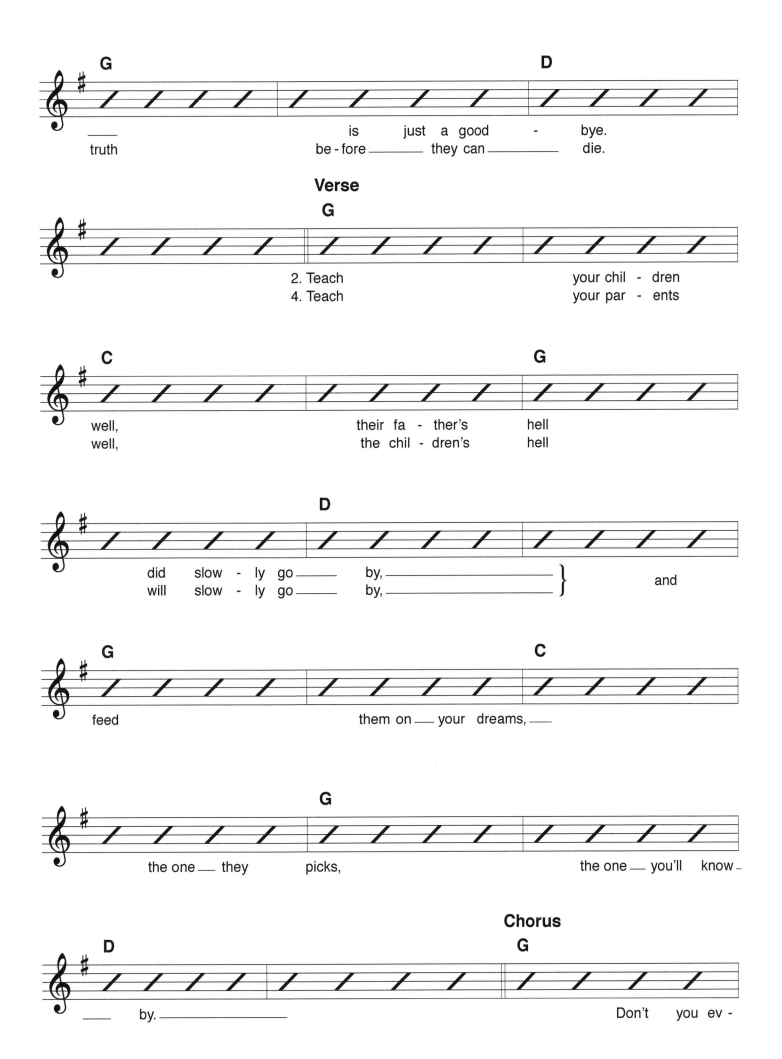

Verse

2. Teach   your chil - dren
4. Teach   your par - ents

well,   their fa - ther's   hell
well,   the chil - dren's   hell

did slow - ly go _____ by, _____ } and
will slow - ly go _____ by, _____

feed   them on __ your dreams, __

the one __ they   picks,   the one __ you'll know __

Chorus

__ by. _____   Don't you ev -

C

-er ask — them why, if they told you, you — would

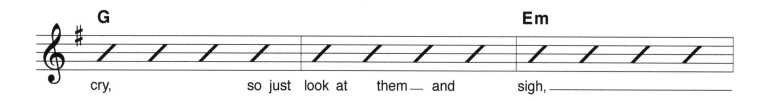

G   Em

cry, so just look at them — and sigh, ——————

C   D

—————————————— and know they

Interlude/Outro

G   C

love ———— you.

1.
G

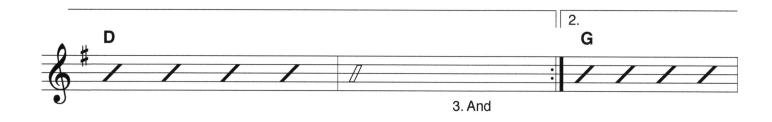

2.
D   G

3. And

D   G   D   G

24

NO WOMAN NO CRY

Words and Music by
Vincent Ford

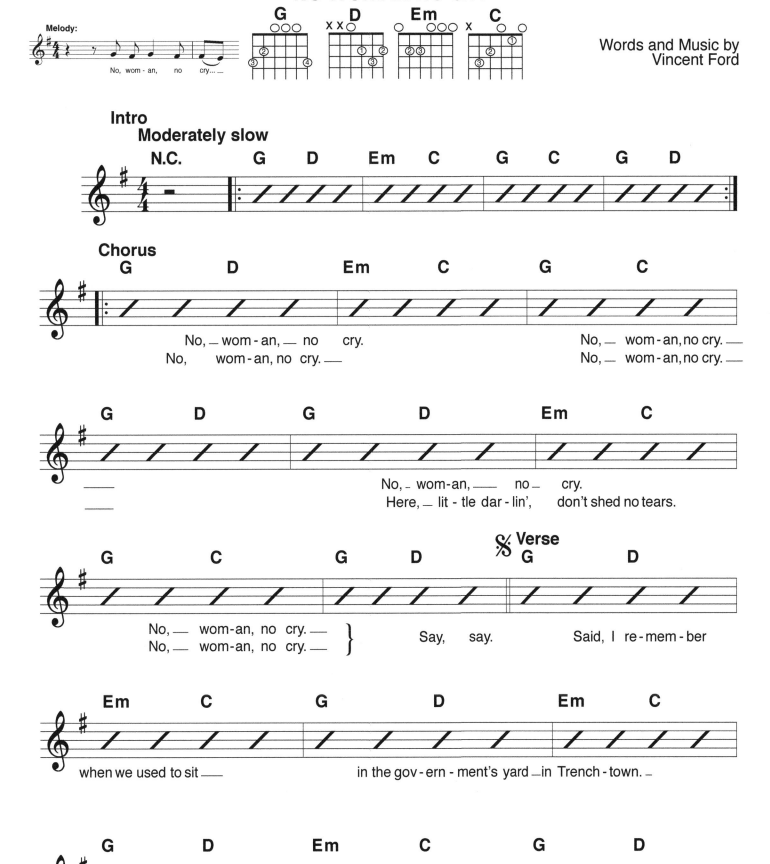

Intro
Moderately slow

Chorus

No, — wom-an, — no cry.
No, wom-an, no cry. —

No, — wom-an, no cry. —
No, — wom-an, no cry. —

No, — wom-an, — no — cry.
Here, — lit-tle dar-lin', don't shed no tears.

No, — wom-an, no cry. —
No, — wom-an, no cry. —

Say, say. Said, I re-mem-ber

Verse

when we used to sit — in the gov-ern-ment's yard — in Trench-town. —

1. O-ba, o-ba, serv-ing the — hyp-o-crites as they would min-gle with the good peo-ple
2.,3. And then Georg-ie would make a fire light, as it was log-wood burn-in' through the

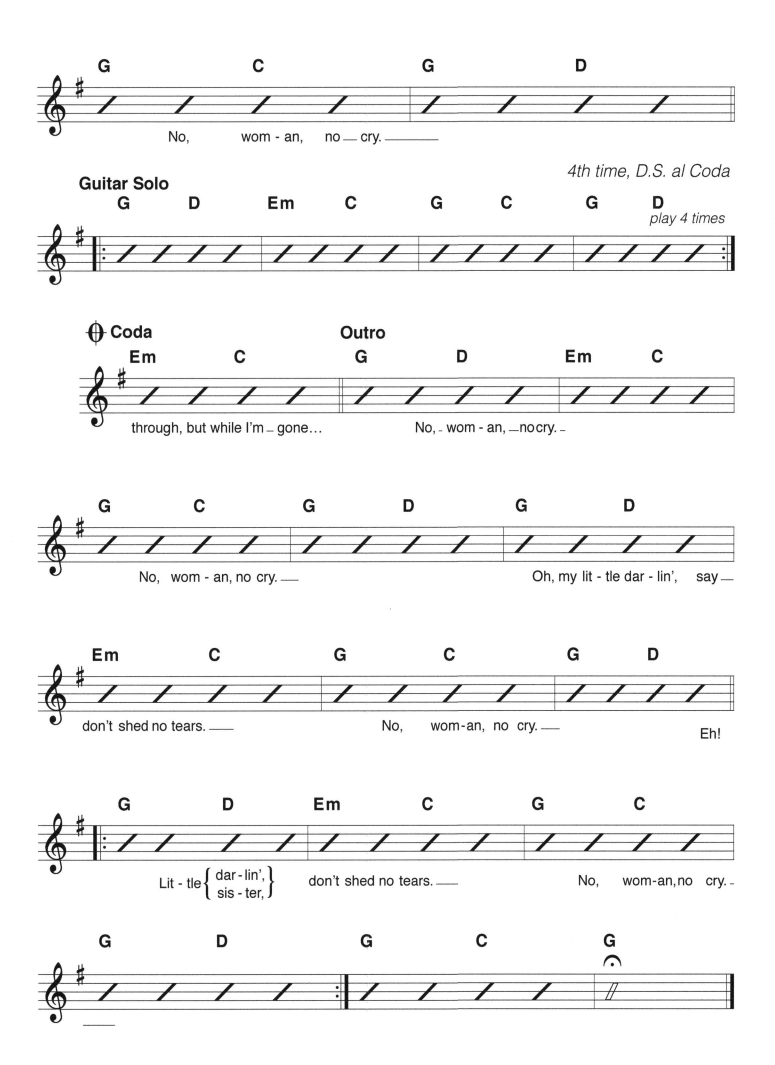

G   C   G   D

No,   wom - an,   no — cry.

4th time, D.S. al Coda

Guitar Solo

G   D   Em   C   G   C   G   D

play 4 times

⊕ **Coda**   **Outro**

Em   C   G   D   Em   C

through, but while I'm — gone…   No, — wom - an, — no cry. —

G   C   G   D   G   D

No,   wom - an, no cry. ___   Oh, my lit - tle dar - lin',   say —

Em   C   G   C   G   D

don't shed no tears. ___   No,   wom-an, no cry. ___   Eh!

G   D   Em   C   G   C

Lit - tle { dar - lin', / sis - ter, }   don't shed no tears. ___   No,   wom-an, no cry. —

G   D   G   C   G

___

LEARNING TO FLY

Words and Music by Tom Petty
and Jeff Lynne

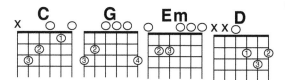

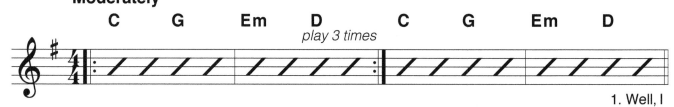

Intro
Moderately

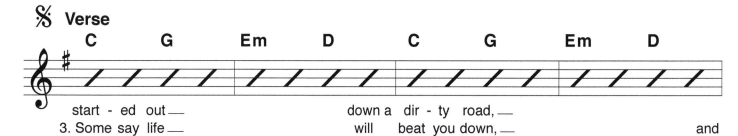

1. Well, I

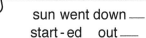 **Verse**

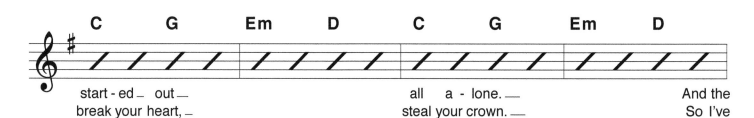

start - ed out ___ down a dir - ty road, ___
3. Some say life ___ will beat you down, ___ and

start - ed _ out ___ all a - lone. ___ And the
break your heart, _ steal your crown. ___ So I've

sun went down ___ as I crossed the hill. ___ And the
start - ed out ___ for God knows where. _ I

town lit up, the world got still. ___
guess I'll know when I get there. ___ I'm

Chorus

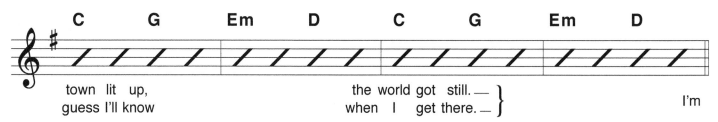

learn-ing to fly ___ but I ain't got wings. ___
a-round the clouds. ___

BROWN EYED GIRL

Words and Music by
Van Morrison

Melody:

Hey, where did we ___ go...

Intro
Moderately

| G | C | G | D |

Verse

| G | C | G | D |

1. Hey, where did we __ go?   Days _ when the rains _ came,
2. Now what - ev - er hap - pened   to Tues - day and so __ slow?
3. *See additional lyrics*

| G | C | G | D |

down _ in the hol - low   play - in' a new _ game,
Go - in' down the old __ mine with a   tran - sis - ter ra - di - o.

| G | C | G | D |

laugh - in' and a run - nin', hey, _ hey,   skip - pin' and a jump - in',
Stand - in' in the sun - light laugh - in',   hid - in' be - hind a rain - bow's wall.

| G | C | G | D |

In the mist - y morn - ing fog _ with   our, our hearts a - thump - in' and you _
Slip - pin' and a slid - in'   all a - long the wa - ter fall _ with you, ___

| C | D | G | Em |

my brown eyed girl. __

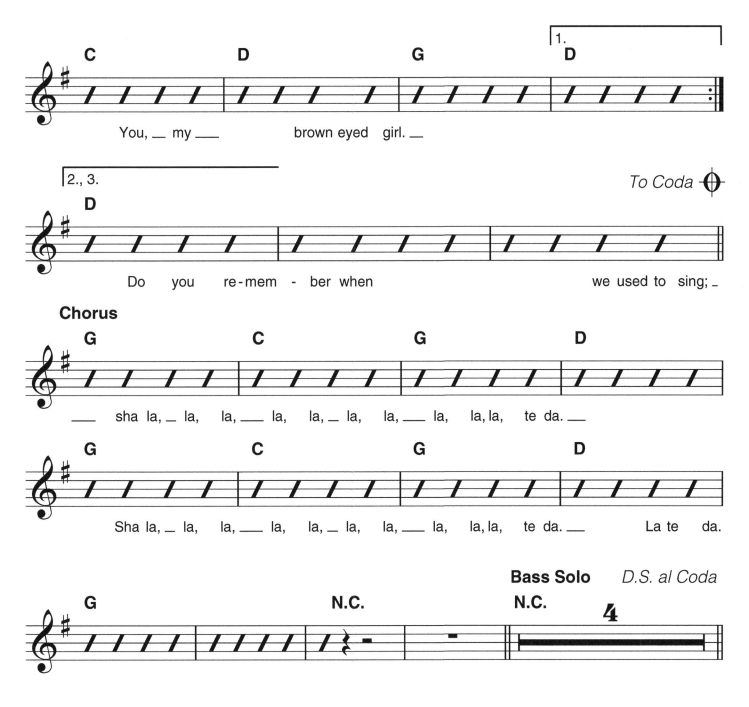

Additional Lyrics

3. So hard to find my way, now that I'm all on my own.
   I saw you just the other day, my, how you have grown.
   Cast my memory back there, Lord,
   Sometimes I'm overcome thinking 'bout it.
   Making love in the green grass
   Behind the stadium
   With you, my brown eyed girl.
   You, my brown eyed girl.
   Do you remember when we used to sing;

HEY, SOUL SISTER

IRIS
from the Motion Picture CITY OF ANGELS

Words and Music by
John Rzeznik

Melody:

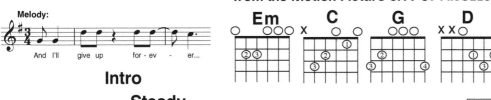

And I'll give up for - ev - er...

Em   C   G   D

Intro
Steady

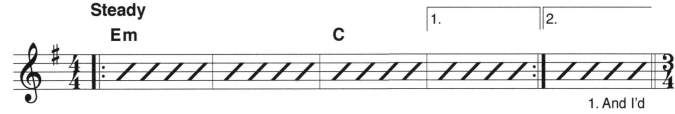

1.   2.

1. And I'd

% Verse

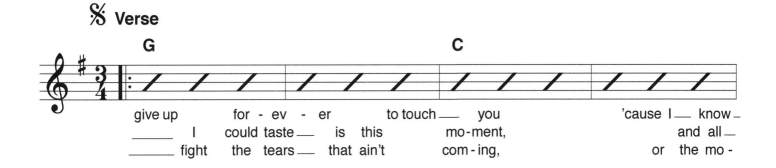

G   C

give up   for - ev - er   to touch ___ you   'cause I ___ know ___
___ I   could taste ___ is   this   mo - ment,   and all ___
___ fight   the tears ___ that ain't   com - ing,   or   the mo -

Em   D   C

that   you   feel _____   me some - how.   You're   the clos -
I   can breathe ___   is   your   life. ___   And
- ment   of   truth ___   in   your   lies. ___   When

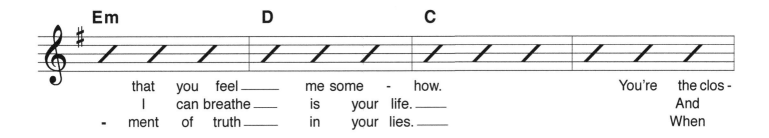

G   C

- est   to heav - en   that I'll _____   ev - er ___ be   and I ___ don't ___
soon-er   or   lat - er   it's o - ver,   I   just   don't ___
ev - 'ry - thing   feels   like   the mo - vies,   Yeah,   you bleed ___

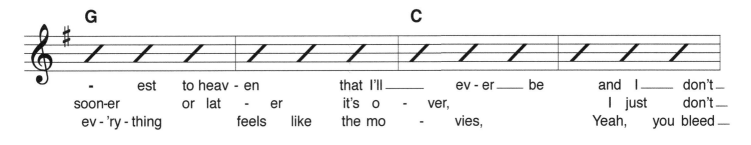

1.   2., 3.

Em   D   C

___ wan - na go ___ home   right   now.   2. And all ___   And I
___ wan - na miss ___   you   to-night. ___
___ just   to know ___   you're   a - live. ___

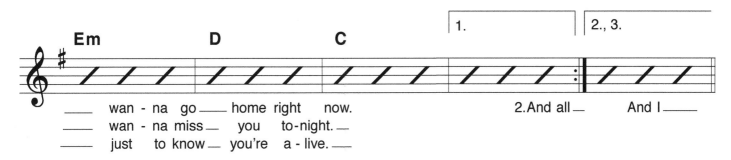

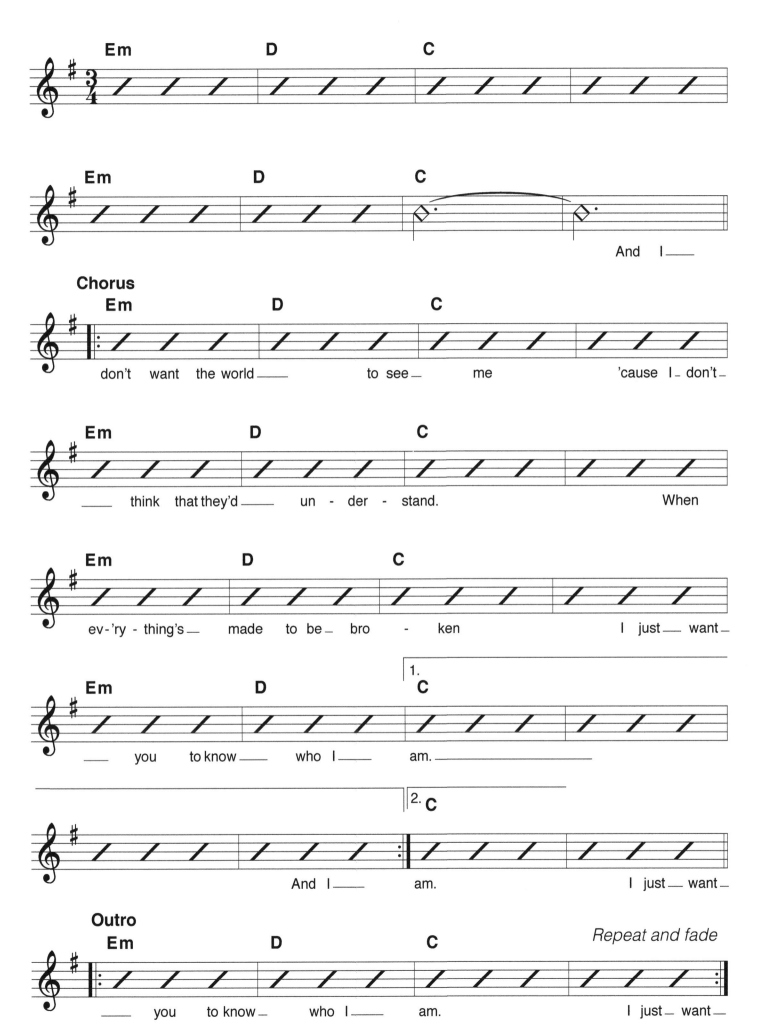

ALL APOLOGIES

Words and Music by
Kurt Cobain

Melody:

What else should I be?...

D   G   A7

Intro
Moderately

key of D

D

Verse

D

1. What else should I be? ____   All a - pol - o - gies. ____
2. I wish I was like you, ____   eas - i - ly a - mused. ____

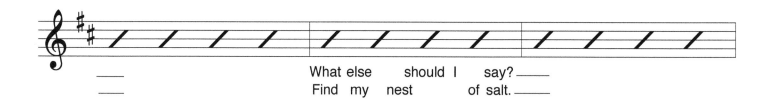

____   What else should I say? ____
____   Find my nest of salt. ____

Ev - 'ry - one ____ is gay. ____   What else should I write? ____
Ev - 'ry - thing ____ is my fault. ____   I'll take all the blame, ____

____   I don't have the right. ____
____   aq - ua sea - foam shame. ____

What else should I be? ____   All a - pol - o - gies. ____
Sun - burn, (with) freez - er - burn. ____   Chok - ing on ____ the ash -

Chorus

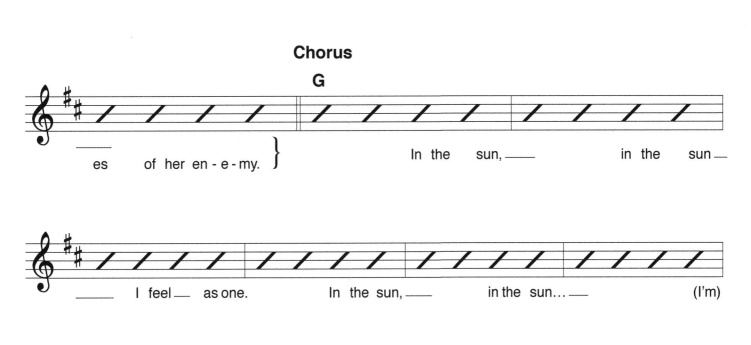

es of her en-e-my.   In the sun, ___   in the sun ___

___ I feel ___ as one.   In the sun, ___   in the sun... ___   (I'm)

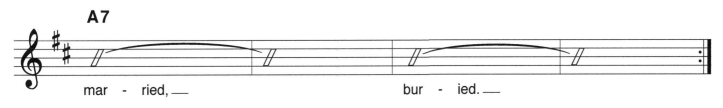

mar - ried, ___   bur - ied. ___

Mar - ried, ___   bur - ied, ___   yeah, yeah, yeah, yeah. ___

Outro

___

All a - lone ___ is all ___   we all ___ are.   All a - lone ___ is all ___

play 6 times   **N.C.**

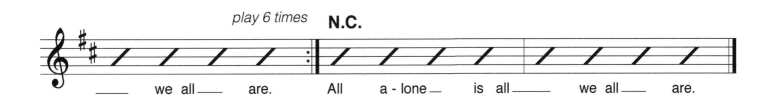

___ we all ___ are.   All a - lone ___ is all ___   we all ___ are.

SURFIN' U.S.A.

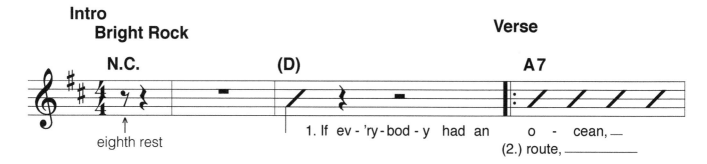

Words and Music by
Chuck Berry

Intro
Bright Rock
Verse

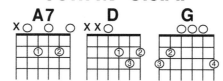

eighth rest

1. If ev-'ry-bod-y had an o- cean, —
(2.) route, —————

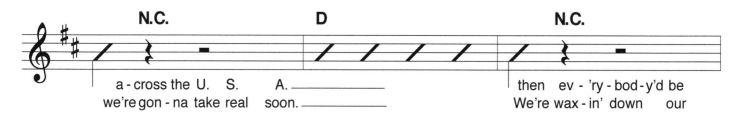

a - cross the U. S. A. —————
we're gon - na take real soon. —————

then ev - 'ry-bod-y'd be
We're wax - in' down our

surf - in' ——
surf - boards, —

like Cal - i - for - ni - a. —————
we can't wait for June. —————

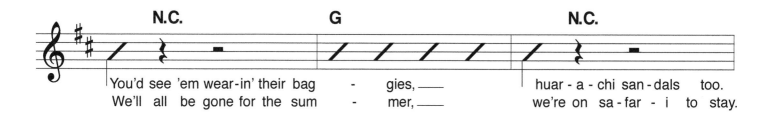

You'd see 'em wear-in' their bag - gies, ——
We'll all be gone for the sum - mer, ——

huar - a - chi san-dals too.
we're on sa-far - i to stay.

A bush - y, bush - y blonde hair - do, ——
Tell the teach-er we're surf - in', ——

sur-fin' U. S. A. —

You'll catch 'em surf - in' at
At Hag - gar - ty's and

TWIST AND SHOUT

Words and Music by Bert Russell
and Phil Medley

Intro
Moderately

Chorus

Well, shake it up ba - by, _ now, (Shake it up ba - by.) twist and

shout. _____ (Twist and shout.) Come on, come on, come on, come on, ba - by now.
(Come on ba -

Come on and work it on out. _____
- by.)
(Work it on out. _____ Oo.)

1. Well, work it on out. _____
2., 3. *See additional lyrics*

Verse

(Work it on out. __) You know you look so good. _____ (Look so good. __

__)You know you got me go - in' now. (Got me goin'. __) Just like I knew you would. __

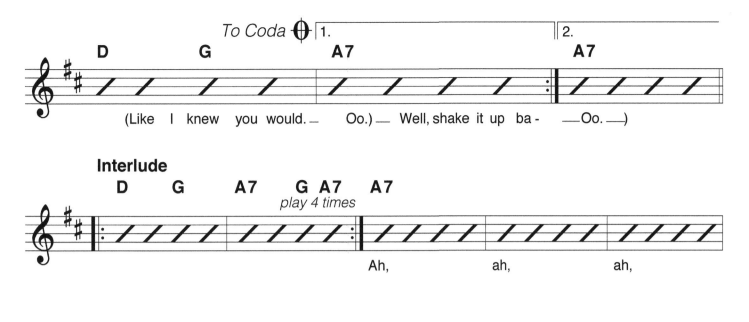

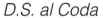

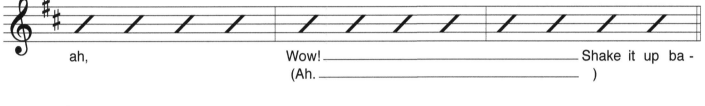

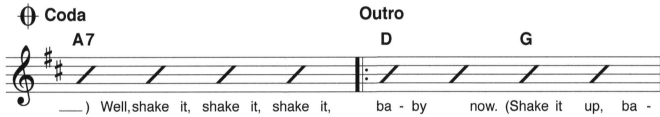

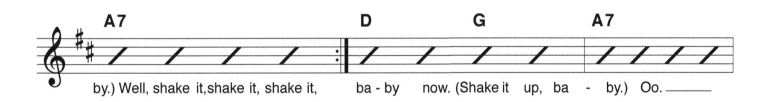

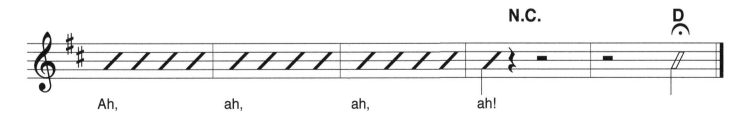

Additional Lyrics

2., 3. You know you twist, little girl.
(Twist little girl.)
You know you twist so fine.
(Twist so fine.)
Come on and twist a little closer now,
(Twist a little closer.)
And let me know that you're mine.
(Let me know you're mine. Oo.)

THAT'LL BE THE DAY

Words and Music by Jerry Allison,
Norman Petty and Buddy Holly

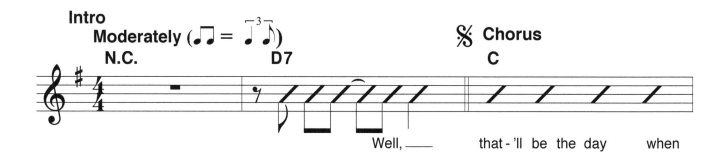

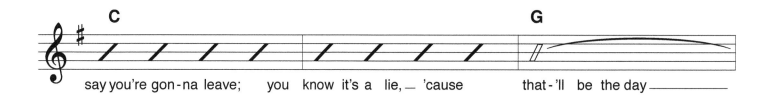

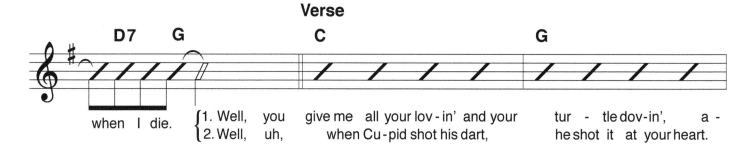

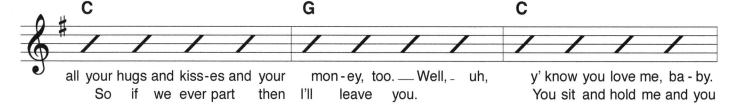

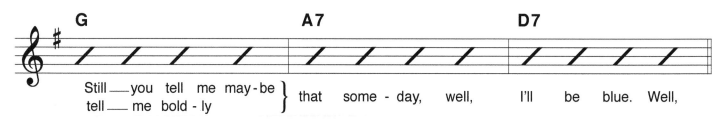

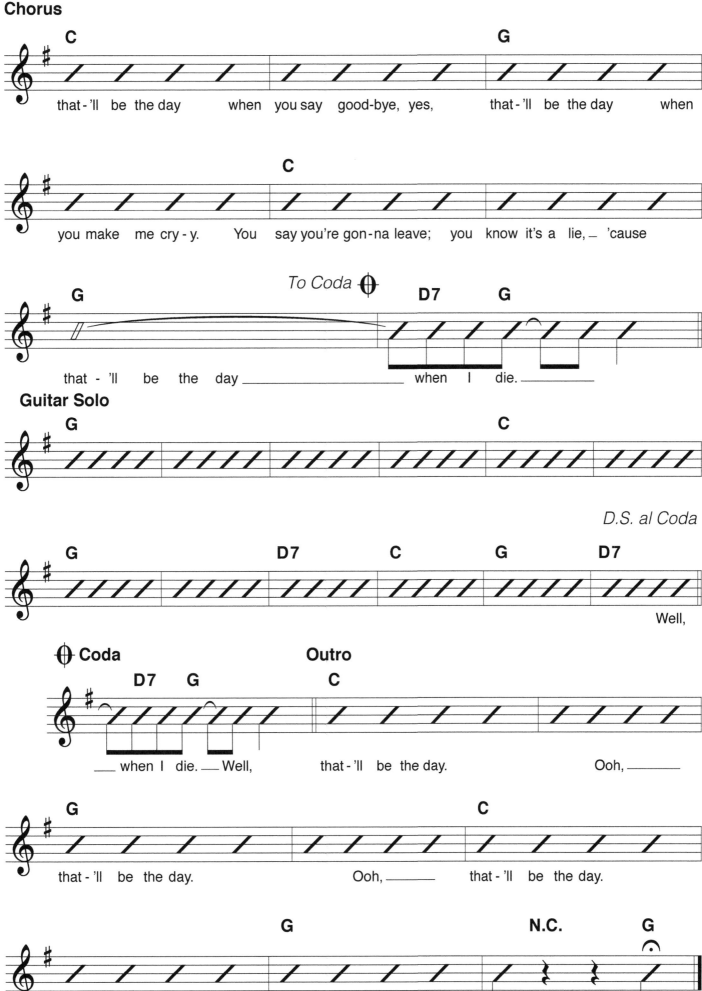

DON'T BE CRUEL
(To a Heart That's True)

Words and Music by Otis Blackwell
and Elvis Presley

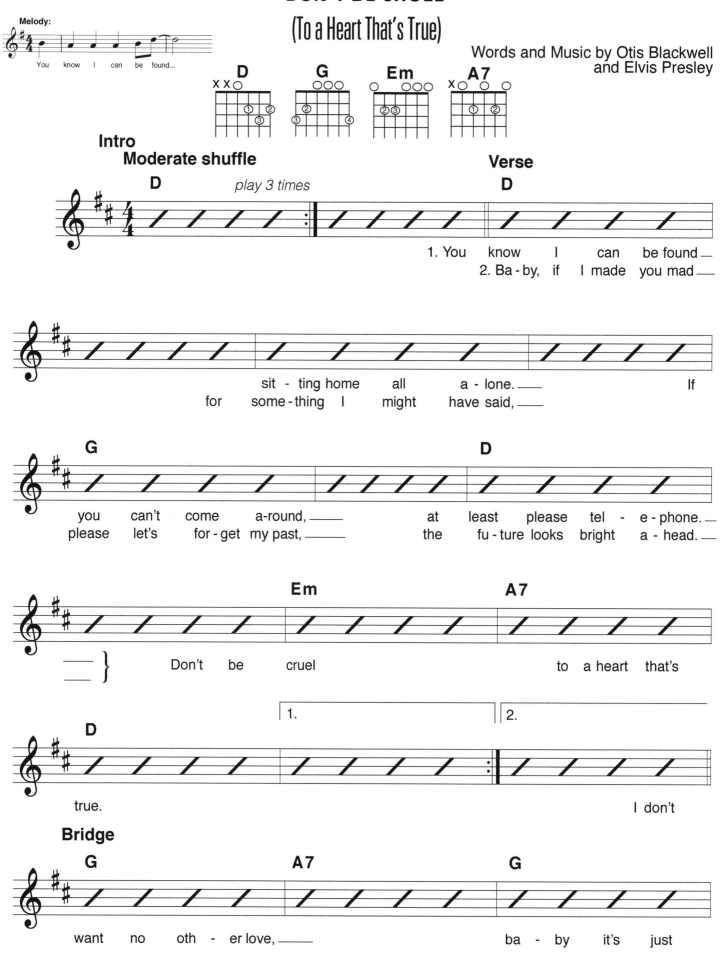

STRUM PATTERNS

The first responsibility of a chord player is to *play the right chord on time*. Keep this in mind as you learn new strumming patterns. No matter how concerned you might be with right-hand strumming, getting to the correct chord with your left hand is more important. If necessary, leave the old chord early in order to arrive at the new chord on time.

That said, here are some suggested strum patterns. Choose one that challenges you, and practice it. Whenever you learn a new chord or progression, try putting it into one of these patterns. Also, try applying these to the songs in this book.

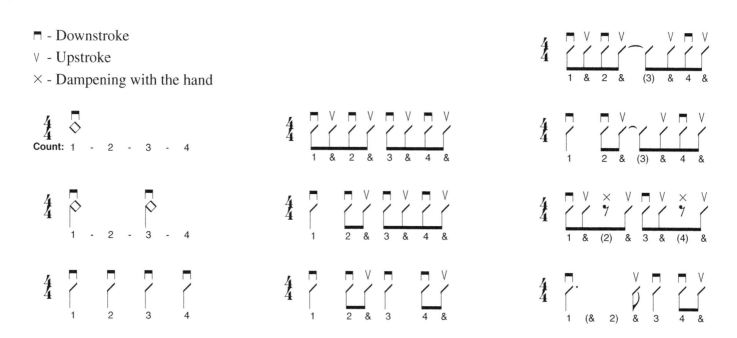

Eighth notes in the above strums may be played even or uneven ("swung") depending on the style of music.

CHORDS

Here are all the chords needed to play the songs in this book.

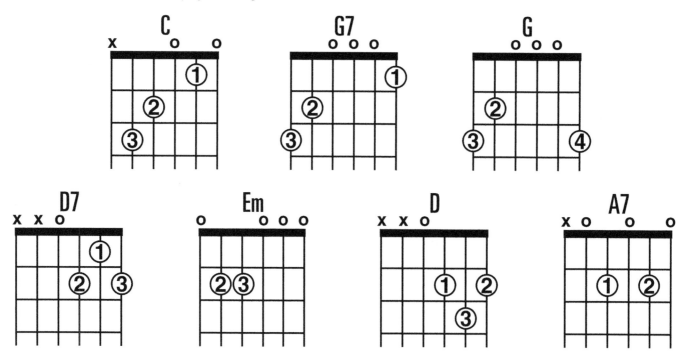

These are presented in the order you learned them in Book 1 of the *Hal Leonard Guitar Method*.